Cups Chint th Car

BRITISH TEA AND
COFFEE CUPS
1745–1940

Steven Goss

D0539715

Published in Great Britain in 2013 by Shire Publications Ltd,
Midland House, West Way, Botley, Oxford OX2 0PH, United Kingdom.
44-02 23rd Street, Suite 219, Long Island City, NY 11101, USA.

E-mail: shire@shirebooks.co.uk   •   www.shirebooks.co.uk

© 2000 and 2008 Steven Goss. First published 2000; reprinted 2002 and 2005. Second edition 2008; reprinted 2010, 2011, 2012 and 2013.

All rights reserved. Apart from any fair dealing for the purpose of private study, research, criticism or review, as permitted under the Copyright, Designs and Patents Act, 1988, no part of this publication may be reproduced, stored in a retrieval system, or transmitted in any form or by any means, electronic, electrical, chemical, mechanical, optical, photocopying, recording or otherwise, without the prior written permission of the copyright owner. Enquiries should be addressed to the Publishers.

Every attempt has been made by the Publishers to secure the appropriate permissions for materials reproduced in this book. If there has been any oversight we will be happy to rectify the situation and a written submission should be made to the Publishers.

A CIP catalogue record for this book is available from the British Library.

Shire Library no. 377   •   ISBN-13: 978 0 74780 695 0

Steven Goss has asserted his right under the Copyright, Designs and Patents Act, 1988,
to be identified as the author of this book.

Designed by Ken Vail Graphic Design, Cambridge, UK, and typeset in Perpetua and Gill Sans.
Printed in China through Worldprint Ltd.

13 14 15 16 17   14 13 12 11 10 9 8 7 6 5

COVER IMAGE
A group of tea and coffee cups from the eighteenth, nineteenth and twentieth centuries. (Author's collection)

TITLE PAGE IMAGE
Caughley coffee can printed in underglaze blue with the Mother and Child pattern, *c.*1785.

CONTENTS PAGE IMAGE
Tea wares by J. & M. Bell of Glasgow, with typical high looping handles and a Scottish landscape view, *c.*1885.
(© H. Jack 1994, courtesy Henry Kelly collection)

ACKNOWLEDGEMENTS
The author would like to thank the following for their generous help with the illustrations for this book: Jackie Marder and Dreweatt Neate Fine Art Auctioneers of Newbury; Jane Bennett and Norfolk Museums Service (Norwich Castle Museum); Gillian Anderson; Keith Ashby; Baron Art of Holt; Bramah Museum of Tea and Coffee; Roger de Ville Antiques; Margaret Drewery; T. W. Gaze & Son of Diss; Goss and Crested China Club; Linzi Goss; Colin House; Heather Jack; Stella McIntyre and the Spode Museum; Sheila Miller; Patrician Antiques of California; Brenda Shortell; R. Twining & Co Ltd; and the private collector who kindly allowed me into her home to photograph pieces from her collection.

CONTENTS

INTRODUCTION

THE arrival in Britain of a strange and exotic drink called tea during the middle part of the seventeenth century was to change the drinking habits of the nation. Introduced into England via the ships of the East India Company, tea was an expensive drink and needed unfamiliar equipment to prepare and drink it. The attractive and delicate porcelain spouted pots and handleless cups brought from China were much admired and tea drinking soon became a status symbol.

There are conflicting theories about how tea was prepared and drunk. One theory is that the leaves were placed in the handleless cup, now known as a tea bowl, and infused by adding boiling water from what we now call a teapot. The saucer was then placed on top of the cup as a cover until the tea was ready. The tea may then have been poured into the saucer to allow it to cool before being drunk. There is probably some truth in the persistent idea that tea was drunk from the saucer, but it is unlikely to have been common practice.

The social importance of tea drinking created a whole new industry and ensured that every utensil associated with the drink, from caddies and spoons

A very early Worcester octagonal coffee cup with C-scroll handle, c.1753. (Dreweatt Neate)

A bill for tea supplied by Twinings, the oldest firm of tea blenders in Britain, founded in 1706. Black tea, made from fermented leaves, and green tea, made from unfermented leaves, were the two main types available. (R. Twining & Co)

Below: The oriental influence on British tea wares. (From left) Early Bow tapering-sided coffee can painted in the 'famille rose' palette and with a handle style also copying the Chinese imported wares of the period, c.1753; Coalport, still using decorations of Chinese landscapes, c.1815; Worcester, depicting oriental figures at a table, c.1765; Bow, painted in coloured enamels showing European flowers, c.1760. Compare this last with the first Bow example – decorators were not familiar with Chinese flowers. (Dreweatt Neate)

to tea tables and trays, would be made to a suitably high standard and would closely follow the latest dictates of fashion. There can be few objects as small as the humble tea and coffee cup which have lent themselves to such variety of shape and decoration and been the subject of so much lavish attention and creative ingenuity.

Coffee reached England in about 1637 and quickly became popular with the opening of coffee-houses, where people could meet and discuss the news of the day. Coffee cups are generally similar to tea cups except that the sides are more upright.

For centuries European potters had tried to emulate the beautiful and lightweight porcelain wares imported from China. The growing fashion of tea drinking, for which earthenware vessels of the time were unsuitable, was ample encouragement for British and European potters to discover the secret of making porcelain themselves.

EARLY WARES

Worcester tea
bowl and saucer
finely 'pencilled' in
black with the Boy
on a Buffalo
pattern, c.1756.
(Dreweatt Neate)

THE formula for hardpaste, or true, porcelain had been known to the Chinese for hundreds of years. Their exports of delicate and finely decorated plates and bowls were the envy of European potters and earthenware manufacturers, whose determination to unravel the secret grew. Although the formula was eventually discovered at Meissen in Germany in the early eighteenth century, it did not reach Britain until about 1760, when an apothecary called William Cookworthy found china clay (kaolin) and china stone (petuntse) in Cornwall and subsequently set up his factory in Plymouth.

These two raw materials are essential to the production of hardpaste porcelain as made by the Chinese, but other would-be porcelain manufacturers were already selling porcelain-type wares which they had developed using various alternative mixes, such as steatite or soapstone, as

a substitute for china clay. These are called softpaste porcelains and the vast majority of all tea wares made in Britain during the eighteenth century are of this type.

The difference between hardpaste and softpaste porcelain is difficult to describe, but hardpaste is fired at a higher temperature, is generally cold to the touch and has a 'glassy' appearance. Softpaste porcelain has a softer glaze and feels warmer to the touch.

Production of softpaste porcelain began in about 1745 at Chelsea and within just a few years there were also factories at nearby Bow, Vauxhall and Limehouse, as well as at Worcester, Derby, Liverpool and several other locations. Tea wares were amongst the first items to be produced and many of the pieces were decorated with oriental scenes, often copied straight from Chinese imports.

There is a reference to the Bow factory in the fourth revised edition of Daniel Defoe's *Tour of Great Britain* written in 1748: '… a large manufactory of porcelain is lately set-up. They have already made large quantities of cups, saucers etc., which by some skillful persons are said to be little inferior to those which were brought from China …'

It was not only the Chinese imports that influenced the early decorators. There was also a strong Japanese influence, with some charming designs being produced in the Kakiemon style. In April 1757 the *Public Advertiser* carried a report of an auction sale '… of the Bow china, and that there will be exhibited large table services of the finest old Japan patterns …'

Softpaste porcelains needed to be glazed as the body would otherwise be porous. The blue and white decoration that is commonly found on

Above left:
A *blanc-de-Chine* coffee cup from the Bow factory, *c.*1755. (Author's collection)

Above right:
Liverpool coffee cups. The bell-shaped cup with scroll handle is painted with a chaffinch on a branch and is from the early Liverpool factory of William Reid, *c.*1758; the other two cups have grooved loop handles, *c.*1765. (Dreweatt Neate)

(Left) Worcester coffee cup and saucer in the Feather Mould Floral pattern, c.1760. (Right) Coffee cup and saucer with a moulded scroll handle from the factory of Richard Champion in Bristol, c.1775. (Dreweatt Neate)

eighteenth-century tea wares was either painted or printed on to the body before it was glazed using the metallic oxide of cobalt. This substance was black when applied and turned blue only after firing, so the painter had to use his skill and experience to judge how the tones and shading would look on the finished article.

Hand painting was the preferred decoration on the elegant tea wares commissioned by the wealthy and titled classes. It is most easily identified where colours are shaded. Brushwork tends to have a freedom and fluidity that cannot be achieved with a print. Popular subjects for hand painting were sprigs and flowers, trailing leaves and oriental scenes with animals, birds and figures.

Transfer-printed decoration is the result of a technique whereby a copper plate is etched, or in later years engraved, with the required design and then

Worcester tea bowl and saucer hand-painted with the Cannonball pattern, c.1770. (Author's collection)

Inset: This disguised numeral mark on a Worcester tea bowl is intended to look like a Chinese character. Concealed within it is the number 7. All numbers from one to nine were disguised in a similar fashion. (Author's collection)

inked with a ceramic pigment. The copper plate is then carefully cleaned to leave only the engraved lines containing pigment. Next a special paper wetted with soap is placed on the copper plate, rolled through a press, peeled off and transferred to the porcelain surface. Once the design was securely in place the paper was washed away. The copper plate could be used many times to produce a high volume of items with an identical pattern at a relatively low cost, especially as it also required only one firing. The process was probably first tried on tea wares at Bow in 1756, but the following year its chief exponent, Robert Hancock, moved to Worcester, where it became widely used, particularly from the 1770s.

Only the cobalt oxide blue could withstand the initial very high firing temperature but other coloured decoration could subsequently be added using various colouring pigments called enamels. Usually mixed on a lead base, they were fired to a second glaze at a lower temperature. The high lead content of the glaze was one of the worst health hazards faced by

Two Worcester cups, *c.*1765. (Left) The Scalloped Peony pattern in underglaze blue; (right) floral decoration in overglaze enamels. (Author's collection)

Typical cups of *c.*1775. The third from left is Liverpool, the others are Worcester. (Private collection)

9

(Left) Lowestoft tea bowl and saucer. (Centre) A tea bowl from the Vauxhall factory. (Right) Liverpool tea bowl and saucer in the Rural Lovers pattern, which is taken from a painting by Gainsborough. (Private collection)

eighteenth- and nineteenth-century potters and lead poisoning was not uncommon.

The Worcester, Liverpool, Lowestoft, Bow and Chelsea factories all produced some fine enamelled tea wares which are highly collectable today. Many of the Worcester designs reflect the influence of the Chinese *famille verte* and *famille rose* porcelains, whereas at Chelsea the influence was more Japanese.

Naturally one might expect factories to decorate all their tea wares in a host of colourful patterns that were pleasing to the eye, but some of the earliest cups and saucers were decorated only with simple moulded flowers and left uncoloured. These charming pieces are known as *blanc-de-Chine*.

Not all cups were decorated at the factory where they were made. Some of the most lavish pieces were painted and gilded by 'outside decorators' such as James Giles, who had a decorating establishment in London. He acquired either white glazed wares or pieces with only some underglaze blue ground colour from factories such as Bow and Worcester and he then

Worcester tea bowls in common patterns. (From left) Fence pattern, Three Flowers pattern, Bandstand pattern, Fisherman and Cormorant pattern. All c.1780–90. (Author's collection)

Two Caughley tea bowls with identical patterns. The smaller bowl is probably an early experimental piece, c.1775. It has firing faults and is barely big enough to accommodate the transfer-printed design, whereas the larger tea bowl was made about ten years later, when production was perfected. (Author's collection)

decorated these to an exceptionally high standard. In particular, the gilding on these pieces is often superior to that of the Worcester factory.

Another independent decorating firm was that of Robert Chamberlain and his son Humphrey. Their workshop was in Worcester and they bought wares 'in the white' from the Caughley (pronounced 'calfley') factory in Shropshire, although by 1791 the Chamberlains were manufacturing fine-quality porcelains of their own.

Many early cups and saucers were unmarked and identifying which factory a piece is from can sometimes be difficult. Some factories, notably Worcester, often marked their cups with oriental-looking seals and characters as if trying to convince the purchaser that the product was every bit as good as those imported from China. Identification is made more difficult because several factories blatantly copied both the marks and the patterns of their competitors. However, in recent years it has been possible to excavate the sites of some of these early factories and the research carried out on the fragments of wasters found has made identification much easier.

The left and centre cups are from the New Hall factory. On the right is a cup from an unidentified factory but decorated with New Hall's Boy and the Butterfly pattern. (Private collection)

Caughley coffee can in the Three Flowers pattern, c.1785. (Author's collection)

Early tea and coffee cups and saucers were relatively small and remained of simple form for many years with the principal area of embellishment to the basic shapes being the handles. By 1780 cups were appearing in new shapes to cater for a growing market. Whereas cups had previously been regarded as a purely functional drinking vessel, they were now starting to become more ornamental and some of the new shapes and patterns were given names. Cups with vertical fluting appeared in about 1780 and remained in fashion for about fifteen years before being joined by shanked or twisted fluting. Customers could now ask for the style of their choice by name and 'New Festoon', 'Blue and Gold Spike' or 'Shanked Cups' could be specified when placing an order.

The coffee can, which looks like a small mug, also became popular in about 1780 although it had been in general production during earlier years. These items were offered as a more expensive alternative to coffee cups and are still generally more expensive to buy today.

So how much did a tea service cost in the eighteenth century? An order book of 1794 from the Chamberlain factory at Worcester lists that a tea service decorated with simple enamelled sprigs on a plain cup shape was £2, while one with a more elaborate pattern on fluted or moulded cups would have cost around £8. A tea service usually comprised a teapot, sucrier (sugar bowl), jug, spoon tray, slop bowl, two cake plates, twelve tea cups, twelve coffee cups and twelve saucers.

Miniature Caughley cup and saucer in the Fisherman and Cormorant pattern next to a standard-size cup. These toy pieces are eagerly sought by collectors. They are not salesman samples as is sometimes thought. (Private collection)

The slop bowl was for putting the used tea leaves and residue into. The saucers were for use with either the tea cups or the coffee cups. This means

that there were many more cups produced than saucers, resulting in a similar disproportion available today. Single cups are therefore often available, but the addition of a matching saucer could add significantly to the price. A collector may see a 'trio' offered for sale and this should comprise a tea cup, a coffee cup and a saucer.

The expanding network of canals resulted in a big reduction in the cost of transport. Ordinary households could now more easily afford to replace their pewter dishes and horn mugs with new china, and the growth in popularity of drinking tea and coffee in the home led to an increase in demand for porcelain tea wares.

Fine-quality Caughley coffee cup and saucer with gilded family crest of a winged eagle on a ducal coronet. (Author's collection)

Coffee can and saucer from the Pinxton factory, hand-painted with a wooded river landscape, c.1800. (Dreweatt Neate)

13

Above:
(From left) A
straight-sided
coffee can from
the Liverpool
factory of Seth
Pennington and
John Part, c.1780;
Caughley coffee
can printed in
underglaze blue
with the Mother
and Child pattern,
c.1785; Worcester
moulded coffee
cup with C-scroll
handle, c.1760.
(Dreweatt Neate)

In 1791 the directors of the East India Company decided to abandon the porcelain trade and the vast shipments of Chinese porcelain ceased. This momentous decision left a void in the market, especially as England was involved in a war in Europe at that time and no European porcelains were being imported either. This shortfall, combined with the recently reduced tax on tea and the imposition of a tax on silver, resulted in an unprecedented demand for tea wares. It was an opportunity that was seized upon and the number of porcelain factories in Britain grew rapidly from 27 operating in the period 1780–90 to 106 in production during the decade 1810–20.

Below: Worcester tea wares in the Waiting Chinaman pattern, c.1770, which have been 'clobbered' by the addition of red, green and gold enamel colours applied over the glaze a few years later. 'Clobbering' is a derogatory term used by collectors for the practice of overpainting an original design. It was a way for manufacturers to make old stock more saleable. The 'sparrow beak' jug is typical of this period; the large slop bowl is for the used tea leaves and residue. (Dreweatt Neate)

NEW SHAPES OF THE EARLY NINETEENTH CENTURY

A T THE BEGINNING of the nineteenth century there were a number of significant developments for tea wares and porcelain production in general. The hardpaste porcelain made at Plymouth, and subsequently at Bristol, had not been hugely successful but by the 1790s the process had been improved and several factories were producing a type of hybrid hardpaste porcelain. By 1815 the process had been perfected and manufacturers were now able to make 'bone china'.

The addition of calcined animal bones strengthened and whitened the body and enabled items to be made with a thinner gauge. The new bone china was also more reliable in the firing process, resulting in fewer losses.

Four cups from c.1800. (Clockwise from top left) Coalport shanked tea cup with an inner spur on the handle; Neale coffee cup; Derby coffee cup in the Hamilton flute shape; slightly waisted and shanked Worcester coffee cup. Gilt rims were popular at this time. (Author's collection)

Pinxton coffee can and saucer decorated with finely painted insects, pattern number 241, c.1810; and a Derby trio with flower-entwined monogram, c.1790. (Dreweatt Neate)

These were distinct improvements and bone china is still the standard British porcelain body made today.

The fashionable cup shapes of the early nineteenth century were the Hamilton flute, which consisted of vertical facets rather than fluting, the royal flute, which had a mixture of wide and narrow panels around the bowl, and the Bute, with its simple and elegant rounded shape.

A new method of printing on ceramics called *bat printing* was sometimes used for decorating cups and saucers at this time. The image is produced on a copper plate using a series of punched dots. Oil was then applied to the plate and the surface oil removed, leaving a residue in the dots. A thin 'bat' of glue or gelatine was then used to transfer the picture in the form of tiny globules of oil. A powdered pigment colour was then dusted on to the oil, which retained the colour for firing. Landscapes were popular subjects for bat printing, which resulted in a much softer image than line engraving. Most bat prints are black but other colours were occasionally used.

Dating cups accurately to within a few years is not as difficult as it might seem. Some styles were produced for just a short period and knowing when

(From left) Miles Mason coffee can painted with ruins within gilt bands and with the addition of a thumb rest on the loop handle; Coalport, decorated in gilt with Greek figures; New Hall with landscapes in gilt panelled bands. All c.1810. (Dreweatt Neate)

Top left: (Clockwise from top left) Coalport tea cup of empire shape; Derby can with an ear handle (seemingly found only with this factory); New Hall tea cup of London shape; New Hall tea cup of Bute shape but with an oval ring handle (often associated with this factory); Machin tea cup of Bute shape with usual ring handle. (Author's collection)

Above: Early nineteenth-century tea sets could be bought with every piece showing different hand-painted scenes. This London shape set is c.1820. (Private collection)

Top right: Davenport coffee cans, c.1810. The one above is earthenware, the other is a white pottery called pearlware, which was initially developed by Wedgwood and became fashionable during the first decade of the nineteenth century. (Dreweatt Neate)

Right: Examples of monochrome decoration. The Coalport can (top) is painted in puce; the Minton can is decorated in blue monochrome, which is more unusual. Both c.1810. (Dreweatt Neate)

Above: A pair of Coalport cans, independently decorated, probably in the London workshops of Thomas Baxter. One depicts Cupid, the other has a putto, emblematic of victory, c.1810. (Dreweatt Neate)

Top right: Spode tea wares, c.1815, painted in gilt with scrolling leaves. The tea cups are Bute shape. (Dreweatt Neate)

Centre right: (Top) Minton, hand-painted in coloured enamels, c.1805. (Front, from left) Possibly Neale, bat-printed landscape, c.1810; Flight, Barr & Barr, finely painted with a named view of Babbacombe Bay on a gilt seaweed ground, c.1815; New Hall, painted in the *famille rose* style, c.1795. Named views are very desirable. (Dreweatt Neate)

Right: Tea and coffee cups in the Etruscan shape, c.1820. (Dreweatt Neate)

Top: Coffee cans showing different handle forms. (Top, left to right) Bloor Derby, with notched loop handle, *c.*1825; Spode, with a handle known to collectors as 'Spode's kinky handle', *c.*1815. (Front, left to right) Minton, with ring handle, *c.*1810; Coalport, with scroll handle, *c.*1815; Coalport, with French handle, *c.*1810. (Dreweatt Neate)

Bottom: Minton coffee cans from a set with different oriental scenes, *c.*1810. (Dreweatt Neate)

a shape was first introduced, combined with other details such as the manufacturer or a pattern number, can enable a cup to be pinned down to a fairly precise date.

For example, embossed floral motifs were introduced in about 1813, as were porringer shape cups. The graceful Paris flute style, with a low moulded body and high handle, was first seen in about 1815 and lasted about ten years. Another introduction was the empire shape, which was in vogue between about 1815 and 1830.

One of the most popular and enduring shapes is the London shape, introduced in about 1812. It has a very distinctive handle with a pointed top and is easily identified. Also with a distinctive handle, shaped like a figure seven and noticeably pointed, is the Etruscan, although this cup shape is found with other handle forms as well. It can be dated quite accurately to the period from 1817 to 1825.

Handles can be an enormous help when trying to identify which factory made a particular cup. In the eighteenth century handles were usually a plain loop with various more ambitious examples along the same theme, but as the nineteenth century progressed a huge variety of shapes and designs were produced, reflecting the remarkable ingenuity and skills of cup designers.

Top: Coffee cans of the period 1800–20 decorated with landscape scenes. (From left) Coalport, with high loop handle; Herculaneum, bat-printed; Machin, bat-printed; Pinxton, painted in puce; another, possibly Pinxton, boldly painted in coloured enamels; unknown, possibly Neale, painted in puce monochrome with silver lustre bands. (Dreweatt Neate)

Middle, red background: (Top, left to right) Chamberlain 'New Gadroon Tournay Shape', c.1820; variation of the bucket shape, c.1820; Hilditch fluted coffee cup, c.1830. (Bottom, left to right) Coalport, London shape, c.1820; Derby, squat bucket-shaped cup with a square or French handle, c.1810. (Norwich Castle Museum)

Middle, blue background: Nantgarw porcelain cups with the distinctive kidney handle associated with this factory, although other manufacturers copied it, c.1815–20. (Dreweatt Neate)

Bottom: This Chamberlain pattern, number 924, is recorded in their pattern list as 'Princess Charlotte's gadroon rose and heartsease wreath of gold, rich', c.1818. (Dreweatt Neate)

As handles were fashioned in moulds, it is by examining the subtle differences between examples that many attributions can be made.

By now the naming of cup shapes had ceased to be a matter of convenience and had become one of policy and, when the fashion changed towards moulded cups in the 1820s, new shapes began to appear at frequent intervals. Unfortunately there was no collaboration between manufacturers and this inevitably resulted in the same shapes being referred to by different names. Furthermore, these names were often chosen quite randomly by the factories.

Some of the most beautifully decorated cups and saucers ever produced were made in the early part of the nineteenth century. With the technique for making bone china perfected and the employment of some remarkably skilled painters and gilders, the quality of decoration from the major factories was very impressive.

Spode, Minton, Coalport, H. & R. Daniel, Wedgwood, Davenport, Chamberlains and Derby were all capable of producing exquisite cups and saucers of the highest quality for their wealthy and titled patrons. Wonderful ground colours were decorated with enamelled fruit, flowers and birds, superbly painted in reserves and richly gilded. Many cups were moulded and the decoration highlighted the moulded pattern for greater effect. *Gadrooning*, a series of raised curves around the rim, was also popular and it was now common practice to decorate the inside of the bowl as lavishly as the outside.

One of the finest exponents of porcelain decoration was William Billingsley, who had painted landscapes at the Pinxton factory before moving to Worcester. It had been his ambition to have his own porcelain factory and in 1813 he started production at Nantgarw in South Wales. The wares were of a very high standard but the percentage of wasters was also high and within a year Billingsley had been compelled to move to the nearby works at Swansea.

The quality of the pieces made at Nantgarw and Swansea made them much sought after by the outside decorators in London. The majority of the items decorated at the factories themselves would have been painted in the Billingsley style, rather than by his own hand. Nantgarw and Swansea cups are not easily found (because both factories were short-lived) and are therefore very collectable today.

Also very desirable for the modern collector are cups and saucers bearing family armorials or crests. Such a tea service would have been specially commissioned by the family concerned and would therefore be unique. In addition, these pieces are likely to be of a very high quality.

Flight, Barr & Barr coffee can and saucer, richly gilded and painted in coloured enamels, c.1810. (Dreweatt Neate)

PATTERN NUMBERS

THE idea of numbering different patterns may seem an obvious practice for a large porcelain manufactory to undertake, but it was not introduced until the 1780s and even during the nineteenth century there were firms producing a substantial output of wares without a pattern numbering system.

Pattern numbers were originally intended to help the manufacturers identify the different designs and to assist with the processes of invoicing and pricing. The factory would keep a pattern book with all its patterns described and coloured alongside their reference number, although even when a factory used such a system there might still be some designs that remained unnumbered.

The first factory to mark its wares with pattern numbers was probably Derby. A reference was made to the Derby pattern 69 in correspondence written in 1784.

The pattern number was painted on to the underside of cups and saucers, though it is important to note that it may not be the only mark to have been added and that not every number found is necessarily a pattern number. Pattern numbers should therefore be considered as just one of several potential clues to be noted when trying to identify which factory was responsible for a particular piece.

The other marks found on the underside of cups and saucers are called tally marks and were applied by the painter either as a personal mark or to represent the work of a group of employees. As workers were likely to be

Empire shape, c.1820; (right) curled and pinched handle, c.1825. (Norwich Castle Museum)

paid for only the perfect finished pieces they had decorated, these marks would be used to keep a tally or total of the items produced by any particular person or group.

Not all pattern numbers are written simply as a number on the piece to be marked. Some have a prefixed or suffixed letter, whilst others are written as a fraction. With a fraction mark such as 1 / 257, for example, the sequence would probably reach 1 / 999 before commencing with a new series 2 / ...

Understanding the ways in which different factories applied their pattern numbers to porcelain tea and coffee cups can be a very useful clue to identification, and a brief but not necessarily infallible guide to the numbering systems used by the major factories follows.

CHARLES BOURNE

Pattern numbers were progressive up to at least 1017 but were written in fractional form under the initials 'CB', although some examples may have only the number.

CHAMBERLAIN

Progressive numbers. Pattern number 700 reached by 1814, pattern 880 by 1820, pattern 1275 by 1830 and pattern 2040 by 1845.

COALPORT

Progressive numbers up to number 999, reached by *c.*1824. Fractional numbers then commenced with 2 / 1. A third series commencing 3 / 1 began *c.*1833, followed by a fourth series *c.*1839. These were followed by fifth, sixth, seventh and eighth series until *c.*1890, when progressive numbers were reintroduced. Numbers were neatly painted in gold, often placed inside the footrim of cups.

Above left:
A solitaire tea service designed for one person, *c.*1820. (Dreweatt Neate)

Above right:
(Top, left to right) Hilditch & Hopwood coffee cup with a notched loop handle, *c.*1845; Chamberlain coffee cup with eagle's head in the handle, *c.*1825. (Bottom, left to right) Alcock lobed tea cup with an unusual handle, *c.*1830; Coalport tea cup in a shape known as Pembroke, *c.*1827. (Norwich Castle Museum)

Right:
Fluted cups with
Old English handles,
c.1830, by Yates
(left) and Coalport.
By this date it was
common practice
for the inside of
the bowl to be
elaborately
decorated. (Author's
collection)

Below right:
Coalport coffee cup
and saucer of net
embossed shape,
c.1830. (Author's
collection)

Below:
A progressive
pattern number
(top) and a
fractional pattern
number. (Author's
collection)

COPELAND & GARRETT

After taking over the Spode factory in 1833 this partnership continued the progressive numbering sequence previously used, commencing at about 5350 and continuing to about 7750.

H. & R. DANIEL

Progressive numbers, small and neatly painted in gold, from about 3600 to at least 8900.

DAVENPORT

Progressive numbers. Pattern number 1000 reached by c.1830 and number 2000 by c.1850. When the factory closed in 1887 pattern numbers had risen to over 6000.

DERBY

Identification is not usually a problem as the pattern number is often painted under the factory mark. Pattern numbers were largely discontinued after 1820.

A hand-painted moulded cup and saucer by H. & R. Daniel in their mayflower shape, c.1830. (Author's collection)

GRAINGER

Progressive numbers up to 2019, which was reached by c.1839. Numbering then restarted, but with the addition of a cross suffix, and stopped at about 2000x c.1845. After this date a new fractional system was introduced starting at number 2/1. Figures were usually painted quite small and often in gold.

HERCULANEUM

This Liverpool factory used progressive numbers which were usually boldly painted in gold. The numbers reached above 1000.

HICKS & MEIGH

Progressive numbers, characteristically painted under the cup handles. However, this means of identification is not totally reliable because other factories, applying their numbers randomly on the pieces, sometimes placed them directly under the handle by chance.

Coffee cans and saucers. The example at the top is from the Herculaneum factory in Liverpool. It appears to be bat-printed but is actually hand-painted. Front left is a Spode moulded can, c.1815. In the centre are a Derby can with a named view, 'On the River Rhone', and an unusual saucer made as a replacement by Davenport, painted in enamel colours in the Derby style, c.1825. The Swansea can and saucer on the right have been printed in black and then boldly picked out in coloured enamels in the Chinese style, c.1818. (Dreweatt Neate)

KERR & BINNS

This partnership took over the Chamberlain factory in Worcester and continued the progressive numbering sequence, from about 5050 to about 7250.

MILES MASON

Progressive numbers, neatly written. Often prefixed with 'N' or 'No'.

MINTON

Progressive numbers up to about 950, often prefixed 'No', were used during the first period of porcelain production (1796–1816). When production began again in 1824 the progressive sequence restarted at number 1, again with the prefix. The numbers had reached 2865 by 1837, 6518 by 1844 and 9999 by 1850. The new-sequence numbers were generally painted in a small and neat fashion.

NEW HALL

Progressive numbers sometimes prefixed 'N' or 'No'. They reached about 1050 by 1815 and probably continued to about 3500.

PINXTON

Progressive numbers, sometimes prefixed with a 'P' and often boldly painted.

RIDGWAY

(Including John Ridgway, but not his brother William.) Before 1815 a simple progressive system was used, then a new fractional system was introduced for tea wares, starting at 2/1. This sequence probably reached 2/9999 in the 1850s and was followed by a new series commencing with 5/1. Often painted in large orange figures.

(Top, left to right) Worcester, Flight, Barr & Barr period footed coffee cup with typical Worcester handle; a tea cup with a handle divided at the top. (Bottom, left to right) An entwined handle on an ogee shape cup; a handle formed as an animal tail on a Bute shape cup. (Norwich Castle Museum)

ROCKINGHAM

Small, neatly painted progressive numbers. Tea wares, when numbered, range between about 430 and 1565. Some fractional numbers were also used under the numerator 2, but not exceeding 2/250.

SPODE

Progressive numbers, usually applied in red. Number 1500 was reached by c.1810, and 3000 by c.1820. When Copeland & Garrett took over the factory in 1833 the pattern numbers had reached about 5350.

Spode pattern book from 1804 showing designs for tea cups. Note the use of exaggerated perspectives to show the inner rim designs and handle shape. (Spode Museum)

These are not the only factories to use pattern numbers and not all pieces produced by a factory listed above will be marked with a number, even if the pattern had been designated one. The reason for this is that some factories marked only the principal pieces in a tea service, such as the teapot or milk jug. A matching cup and saucer with only one or other bearing a pattern number can often be found.

The same pattern might be used by several factories, each giving it a different number. When a design became popular other manufacturers would copy it, enter it into their own pattern books and allocate the next available number to it. There was also a large trade in producing replacement pieces and a factory could receive an order to supply a cup to match an existing service from another maker but in a pattern it did not already produce, thus requiring an addition to its pattern book.

Tea wares from the Nantgarw factory in South Wales, beautifully painted with flowers, leaves and gilt anthemions, 1814–22. The kidney-shaped handles are typical of Nantgarw cups. (Dreweatt Neate)

THE LATER NINETEENTH CENTURY

Tᴴᴱ number of porcelain manufacturers in business during the 1840s had gone up from 106 in 1820 to 163 but, whilst the volume of tea wares being made rose, the overall quality fell. Some fine pieces were still being made, especially at the leading factories. Minton, Coalport and others made moulded 'net embossed' cups during the 1830s and continued their high standard of output. Davenport, Rockingham and Copeland & Garrett also made some excellent cups during this period.

A new shape called the Adelaide, with a distinctive type of ringed handle, was introduced in about 1830 and remained fashionable for about fifteen years. Pedestal cups, with the bowl raised upon a deep foot, were popular during the middle part of the century.

So far there has been no mention of porcelain made in Scotland or Northern Ireland. The notable firm of J. & M. Bell of Glasgow was amongst the many factories to exhibit at the Great Exhibition in 1851, where it received an honourable mention. Some of its tea wares are of a tall, classic form with high handles and often beautifully decorated with Scottish landscape views.

The Belleek factory in County Fermanagh is perhaps best known for its intricate woven basketware but it produced some fine tea wares as well, with many pieces having the distinctive pearly glaze associated with this factory.

(Left to right) John Ridgway tea cup of union wreath shape, c.1835; Spode with D-handle, c.1826; John Ridgway waisted cup with a broken loop handle, c.1835; Alcock tea cup of Adelaide shape with D-handle, c.1840. Note the moulding on the foot, which may have been painted if the cup had been decorated with a different pattern number. (Author's collection)

Top: (Top, left to right) Copeland & Garrett printed design, c.1845; cup with the handle formed as a snake's head. (Bottom, left to right) Coffee cup with another variation of the D-handle, c.1835; moulded coffee cup of Dresden shape, c.1825; miniature cup of London shape by Copeland & Garrett, c.1845. (Norwich Castle Museum)

Middle: A selection of footed or pedestal cups with a variety of different handle shapes. The centre cup is Copeland & Garrett's Berlin embossed shape and has a Lowther handle, c.1846. (Norwich Castle Museum)

Bottom: Belleek cups with typical pearly glaze on the tea cup. Moulded basketware design with rustic handle painted in natural colours. Late nineteenth century. (Author's collection)

Top: A very fine tea cup and saucer from the Kerr & Binns partnership at Worcester, c.1855. (Dreweatt Neate)

Middle: A tea set designed for two people. These services are known as 'cabaret' sets and were ideal for use in the bedroom or dressing room. This one is by Royal Worcester and has date marks for 1863. (Dreweatt Neate)

Bottom: An unusual Minton tea service, bat-printed with a named view of Barthomley Church. Ordered from Minton by Lady Isabella Spencer in 1867 as a gift for Mrs Norton, it is a copy of a service first produced for Lady Isabella in 1854. Researching the history of pieces purchased can be very rewarding. (Dreweatt Neate)

The Kerr & Binns partnership at Worcester (1851–62) and Brown-Westhead, Moore & Co (1861–1904), which took over the factory previously occupied by John Ridgway at Hanley in Staffordshire, are also noted for the quality of their porcelain at a time when many firms were producing cups of a mediocre standard.

During the late 1870s some factories began designing naturalistic cup styles influenced by the Aesthetic Movement. These cups have coloured and moulded flowers, leaves and tendrils on a plain ground and may also have a brown twig-like handle. Stylish cups of this calibre had their designs registered at the Patent Office. Look for the diamond-shaped registration mark which was used between 1842 and 1883. Cups marked with registration numbers, written 'Rd. No.' followed by the number itself, date from 1884 onwards.

Above: A diamond-shaped design registration mark, used between 1842 and 1883. (Author's collection)

Above left: Naturalistic styles. The cup styled as a cauliflower is Wedgwood, the others are Belleek. (Norwich Castle Museum)

Bottom: Foley China Works cup and saucer, commemorating the Diamond Jubilee of Queen Victoria in 1897. Four years later the same cup shape was used to record her death. (Linzi Goss)

The mark 'England' signifies a date after 1890, and any cups stating 'Made in England' or 'bone china' are of twentieth-century manufacture.

Before leaving discussion of the nineteenth century one further innovation must be mentioned, namely the moustache cup. These cups were specially designed for men who followed the fashion for growing a moustache but who still wanted to drink with dignity. They have an additional shaped piece across the top of the cup to protect the moustache from the liquid. As most people are right-handed, a moustache cup designed for a left-handed drinker is somewhat rarer.

Above:
A late-Victorian moustache cup. (Margaret Drewery)

Right:
Cups depicting local scenes make an interesting collecting theme. These black-printed cups and saucers show various views of Weymouth and Portland in Dorset. (Colin House)

Lower right:
A Maw & Co invalid feeding cup designed to give liquid foods to bedridden patients, c.1890. Patients drank beef tea or a mixture of diluted milk and flour called pap. (Author's collection)

THE EDWARDIAN AND
ART DECO PERIODS

THE ART NOUVEAU style of the late nineteenth century did not have a great influence on cup design but it did make popular the use of modern materials and techniques. The desire for craftsmanship continued during the art deco period which followed.

The Royal Worcester factory (as it was now known) produced exceptionally fine tea and coffee cups, often in cased sets, hand painted in enamel colours and with gilded interiors. The painting was executed by skilled artists, who often signed their work, making it possible to identify exactly who was responsible for the decoration of a particular piece.

Artists would often paint their own specialist subjects. Harry Davis painted animals and game birds, Richard Sebright painted fruit, and John and Harry Stinton both painted Highland cattle. Their work is extremely desirable but they were by no means the only artists of note working at the Royal Worcester factory, and any signed cups and saucers are likely to be expensive purchases today.

The coffee can, which had become popular in the 1780s but which had gone out of favour by about 1820, enjoyed a revival during the inter-war

A set of four Royal Worcester small tea cups, beautifully hand-painted and gilded. Always look for the artist's signature on cups like these. They date from 1920. (Dreweatt Neate)

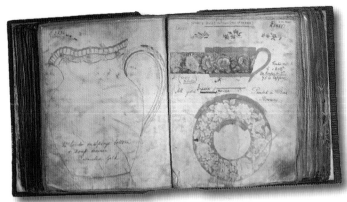

Left:
Spode pattern book from 1909. The factory archives contain over 70,000 recorded patterns. This method of illustrating a wrap-around design is still used today. (Spode Museum)

Right:
Late-Victorian styles, including a pleasing example by George Jones (top left). The large cup by Cauldon China (top right) is called a breakfast cup and is designed to hold the equivalent of two standard tea cups. (Brenda Shortell)

Right:
(Left to right) Shelley 'dainty white' decorated as a souvenir from Llandudno; a delicate shamrock design from the Foley China Works; Phoenix ware art deco cup. (Brenda Shortell / Linzi Goss)

years of the twentieth century. Coffee cans were now smaller and neater and were used for drinking the stronger espresso-type coffees served after a meal.

During the early years of the twentieth century manufacturers were generally rather cautious with the decoration they applied to tea wares. It had been a difficult time for British manufacture and few factories seemed willing to be too adventurous, but some of the smaller firms were prepared to embrace the fashionable styles of art deco, producing pieces that were more distinctive than the rest.

One of these firms was Shelley, which had already introduced a popular fluted style called 'dainty white' in 1896 and was to continue at the forefront of cup design throughout the art deco period. Each cup shape the firm produced was given a name, such as Vogue, Eve or Regent, which it marketed to an increasingly fashion-conscious public through the equally fashionable 'Shelley Girl', who appeared in newspaper and magazine advertisements. Many of the Shelley styles were designed by Eric Slater, whose father was the company director. He had trained at the School of Art in Stoke-on-Trent under the influential Gordon Forsyth.

Favoured motifs during the art deco period were squares, diamonds, crescent moons, oblongs, stars and polka dots. Lustre decoration was also popular. All of these characteristics may be seen in the cups of Susie Cooper, who worked as a designer and decorator for A. E. Gray & Co.

Top:
Crested china was a popular souvenir for travellers. The most notable manufacturer was W. H. Goss, who saw the potential market when railways enabled people to take day trips and holidays. (Goss and Crested China Club)

Bottom:
The two small cups in the centre are demitasse coffee cups. The tea cup on the left is by Royal Albert; the other is Copeland, slightly faceted and well gilded, with rope and tassle decoration. (Author's collection)

Susie Cooper also trained in Stoke-on-Trent under Gordon Forsyth and had been influenced and encouraged by his vision of new designs endorsing simplicity of form and decoration. She began by producing geometric and cubist designs in brilliant colours, but by 1933 her designs had changed considerably, and she was producing cups in simple but elegant styles made of earthenware and decorated in pastel colours.

The name most associated with art deco ceramics is that of Clarice Cliff. Her daring designs and vibrant colours were both innovative and futuristic. Her Bizarre range lived up to its name when it was first offered to an unsuspecting public, who had not seen anything quite like it before. Combining bold geometric designs with continental-looking shapes made of earthenware, it was a huge commercial success.

Left: A tea service designed for children. These nurseryware pieces have pictures and phrases from popular children's stories or nursery rhymes. (T. W. Gaze & Son)

Above: A novelty tea cup and saucer decorated with the signs of the zodiac. (Bramah Museum of Tea and Coffee)

Left: Four cups by Susie Cooper. (Clockwise from top left): Banded, plain, Blue Orchid and Tiger Lily. All 1930s. (Baron Art)

Top: An art deco cup and saucer by Meakin with typical angular handle of the early 1930s. (Norwich Castle Museum)

Middle: (Top) Maling apple-green lustre set, ideal for tea and biscuits, c.1935. (Bottom, from left) Wedgwood, c.1930; Minton, c.1915; Cauldon China coffee can in a silver holder, 1923; Bishop & Stonier, c.1937. (Baron Art)

Bottom: Early designs by Clarice Cliff. (Top, left to right) Bizarre Autumn Crocus Conical shape tea cup and coffee can; Bizarre Autumn Orange. (Bottom) Marguerite tea cup with filled-in flower handle; Viscaria conical shape. All hand-painted, c.1930. (Baron Art)

Further designs followed, including the Conical range, introduced in 1929, which has the solid triangular handles that are the very essence of the art deco tea and coffee cup. Her tea wares are usually clearly marked with her name and she cleverly used her image as a trendy, bright young designer alongside her own 'designer label' as a very effective marketing tool, adding greater prestige to her products.

Some of the other factories producing interesting tea wares of quality during the 1920s and 1930s were Aynsley, Wedgwood, Minton, Belleek, Royal Doulton, Cauldon, Burgess & Leigh (Burleigh) and E. Brain & Co (Foley China Works).

The end of the art deco period and the onset of a second world war marked the closing of an era in which design and craftsmanship had flourished. Whilst manufacturers may still search for new designs to cater for the ever-changing demands of society, some of the shapes discussed in earlier chapters of this book are still in production today.

Above left: Motto ware. Cups with phrases written in a rural style were produced by potteries in the south-west of England, most notably the Watcombe pottery near Torquay. (Brenda Shortell)

Above right: Gypsy Theresa's fortune telling cup. The manufacturer is unknown but it appears to date c.1930. Residue tea leaves were probably used to make the prediction. (Gillian Anderson)

Right: (From left) Burgess & Leigh (Burleigh) art deco coffee cup of zenith shape, c.1931; Minton barrel-shaped cup with a ridged base that fits quite perfectly into the saucer, a sign of good quality, c.1937; Newhall cup of Diana shape, c.1934. (Author's collection)

COMMEMORATIVE CUPS

COMMEMORATIVE cups are those produced for sale (or sometimes given away) that carry a design or shape commemorating a special royal, historical, political, social or sporting event, and are made at the time of the occasion in response to public demand. They were often cheaply produced to satisfy the mass market they were aimed at.

It is worth noting the distinction between a souvenir and a commemorative mug. Although many commemorative pieces may have been bought as souvenirs, by definition a commemorative relates to a specific dated event, whereas a souvenir does not.

The fashion for ceramic commemoratives first appeared in Britain when potters produced mugs and other items bearing the date and portrait of King Charles II to celebrate the restoration of the monarchy in 1660. Since that time pottery and porcelain mugs and cups have been used to mark all kinds of events.

By far the most commonly found commemoratives are those relating to royalty. Coronations and jubilees dominate this popular collecting field, but occasionally a cup with a different royal theme may be found. The one

Bute shape memorial cup for Princess Charlotte Augusta of Wales, who died in childbirth in 1817. She was very popular and was deeply mourned by the whole country. (Patrician Antiques)

Above left:
Two Staffordshire commemoratives recording the coronation of George IV in July 1821. His estranged wife, Caroline of Brunswick, travelled to Westminster for the event, but was turned away at the doors. (Roger de Ville Antiques)

Above right:
A very rare memorial commemorative for Frederick, Duke of York, who died in 1827. He was the heir to the throne and Commander-in-Chief of the British Army, but was always unsuccessful in battle. After a failed campaign in Flanders he was unfairly ridiculed in the nursery rhyme 'The Grand Old Duke of York'. (Roger de Ville Antiques)

illustrated, mourning the death of Princess Charlotte in 1817, portrays a fascinating historical event. She was the only child of the ill-fated marriage between George IV (the Prince of Wales at that time) and Caroline of Brunswick and had an extremely difficult childhood. In 1816 she married Prince Leopold, and when she became pregnant the following year the entire country took a keen interest, but her child was stillborn and the 21-year-old princess died of haemorrhage and shock a few hours later. The nation plunged into grief at the news, and three months later her obstetrician committed suicide, unable to bear the burden of responsibility for the death of the heir to the throne.

Political commemoratives are also very popular and usually record election campaigns and victories, political causes, Acts of Parliament, or deaths. Most items relate to an individual politician.

A rare Staffordshire transfer-printed commemorative celebrating the coronation of William IV in September 1831 and members of the Reform. (Roger de Ville Antiques)

A rare cup commemorating Queen Victoria's succession to the throne in 1837 at the age of eighteen. (Colin House)

Top:
A Staffordshire puce-printed cup and saucer portraying Father Mathew administering the pledge, c.1850. He travelled widely throughout Ireland, England and America and these pieces were sold to commemorate his visits. (Colin House)

Middle:
A transfer-printed cup with gilt inscription 'Harriet E Preston, Dec 27th 1890'. Probably a Christening cup. (Author's collection)

Bottom left:
The gilt inscription on this cup records the death of Richard Blaydes who died on 8 September 1879 at the age of twenty. (Sheila Miller)

Bottom right:
Queen Victoria's Diamond Jubilee in 1897 was a double celebration and cause for a great many commemorative items. The design printed on this unusual tin cup records that her sixty-year reign is also the longest in English history. (Formerly in the author's collection)

Top left:
A Doulton cup and saucer commemorating the death of Queen Victoria in 1901. (Colin House)

Top right:
This cup was made to commemorate the coronation of Edward VII to be held in June 1902. The event was postponed when the King fell ill with appendicitis so Royal Doulton added an inscription declaring the postponement until August. (Colin House)

Middle right:
A simple transfer-printed cup and saucer made by W. H. Goss in 1905 to commemorate the centenary of Nelson's death. (Colin House)

Bottom:
A cup and saucer made by Grafton China to commemorate the Franco-British Exhibition held in London in 1908. (Keith Ashby)

Cups commemorating military personalities and battles such as Balaclava, Sebastopol, or Nelson's victory at Trafalgar are regularly found. There are also many designs celebrating peace at the end of World War I, but cups commemorating scientific discoveries or engineering and sporting achievements are much harder to find.

One of the joys of collecting commemorative cups is discovering more about the events and personalities depicted. A good example of this is the cup and saucer showing Father Mathew and dating to the middle of the nineteenth century. Father Mathew was an Irish temperance reformer who established the Abstinence Society in 1838. His aim was to keep people sober by inviting them to take The Pledge:

> I promise to abstain from all intoxicating drinks except used medicinally and by order of a medical man, and to discountenance the cause and practice of intemperance.

During the 1840s his movement enrolled millions of people across England, America and his native Ireland, and statues are dedicated to his memory in Dublin and Cork.

As mass production increased during the nineteenth century so did the quantity of commemorative wares. A cup celebrating Queen Victoria's coronation would be quite rare, but those recording her death are plentiful.

The large number of visitors to major Exhibitions made them an ideal subject for the sale of mass-produced commemorative wares. The Franco-British Exhibition held in 1908 celebrated the *Entente Cordiale* signed by the United Kingdom and France in 1904 and was the first international exhibition organised and sponsored by two countries. All the exhibition areas

Top left:
A West Country commemorative given by C. E. Parke to the children of Sturminster Marshall in Dorset to celebrate the coronation of George V in 1911. (Colin House)

Top right:
An extraordinary demonstration of ceramic painters' skill. The five medals in the centre of this crest bear inscriptions which were painted with a single hair. (Spode Museum)

Two scarce commemoratives that would have been produced in small numbers. A small Minton mug to commemorate the coming-of-age of the Hon. Edward Llewelyn R. N. Mostyn in 1906, and another marking 600 years of worship at the present church in Wolverton, Warwickshire, between 1316 and 1916. (Colin House)

were painted white, and the area of London where it was held became known as White City. In 1924 the British Empire Exhibition attracted more than seventeen million visitors.

Some commemoratives, such as those marking a family event, would have been made in very small numbers. Despite their scarcity, they are usually of little interest or value beyond the family concerned, although it can be enjoyable to delve into the family's history in an attempt to discover more.

Not all commemorative cups bear a manufacturer's mark, but from the late-Victorian period onwards the better-quality examples usually do. Among the more prolific companies producing commemorative cups were Royal Doulton, Aynsley, Goss, Paragon, Grafton and Bishop & Stonier.

Wares celebrating peace at the end of World War I, including a Bishop & Stonier mug (top right) presented to local children by Samuel Samuel, the MP for Putney. (Bottom, left to right) Small mugs by Osborne China, Aynsley and W. H. Goss. (Colin House)

Top left: 'The Uncrowned King'. A Hammersley piece made in 1936 for the coronation of Edward VIII, who unexpectedly abdicated before the event. His brother succeeded to the throne as George VI and is commemorated with his queen, Elizabeth, by this coronation pair. (Colin House)

Top right: This Royal Stafford cup has an unusual double loop handle. It commemorates the launch of RMS *Queen Mary* in 1936, the largest passenger ship of her day. (Author's collection)

Left: Wares commemorating the coronation of King George VI on 12 May 1937 by Paragon China (top) and Royal Doulton. (Colin House)

FURTHER READING

Berthoud, Michael. *A Compendium of British Cups*. Micawber Publications, 1990.

Branyan, Lawrence; French, Neal; and Sandon, John. *Worcester Blue and White Porcelain, 1751–1790*. Barrie & Jenkins, 1981.

Buckrell Pos, Tania. *Tea and Taste: The Visual Language of Tea*. Schiffer Publishing, 2004.

Burdess, Sheryl. *Shelley Tea Ware Patterns*. Schiffer Publishing, 2003.

Casey, Andrew. *Susie Cooper Ceramics: A Collectors' Guide*. Jazz Publications, 1992.

Cushion, John and Margaret. *A Collector's History of British Porcelain*. Antique Collectors' Club, 1992.

Flynn, Douglas, and Bolton, Alan. *British Royalty Commemoratives*. Schiffer Publishing, revised edition 1999.

Godden, Geoffrey. *Staffordshire Porcelain*. Granada Publishing, 1983.

Godden, Geoffrey. *Encyclopaedia of British Pottery and Porcelain Marks*. Barrie & Jenkins, 2003.

Godden, Geoffrey. *English Blue and White Porcelain*. Antique Collectors' Club, 2004.

Green, Richard, and Jones, Des. *The Rich Designs of Clarice Cliff*. Rich Designs, 1995.

Hill, Susan. *The Shelley Style*. Jazz Publications, 1990.

Lockton, Peter. *Royal Commemorative Mugs and Beakers*. Tuckwell Press, 2007.

Mawston, Colin. *British Art Deco Ceramics*. Schiffer Publishing, 2000.

McKeown, Julie. *Burleigh. The Story of a Pottery*. Richard Dennis, 2003.

Pettigrew, Jane. *The Social History of Tea*. National Trust, 2002.

Pettigrew, Jane. *Designed for Tea*. Sutton Publishing, 2004.

Preller, Pat. *New Hall Porcelain Pattern Book*. Privately printed, 2003.

Smith, Sheenah. *Lowestoft Porcelain in Norwich Castle Museum* (two volumes). Norwich Museum Services, 1975 and 1986.

Twitchett, John. *Derby Porcelain 1748–1848: An Illustrated Guide*. Antique Collectors' Club, 2002.

Watney, Bernard. *Liverpool Porcelain of the Eighteenth Century*. Richard Dennis, 1997.

Wilkinson, Vega. *Spode-Copeland-Spode: The Works and Its People 1770–1970*. Antique Collectors' Club, 2002.

PLACES TO VISIT

The Allen Gallery, 10–12 Church Street, Alton, Hampshire GU34 2BW.
Telephone: 0845 603 5635.
Website: www.hants.gov.uk/museum/allen
Bramah Museum of Tea and Coffee, 40 Southwark Street, London SE1 1UN.
Telephone: 020 7403 5650. Website: www.teaandcoffeemuseum.co.uk
Derby Museum and Art Gallery, The Strand, Derby DE1 1BS.
Telephone: 01332 716659.
Website: www.derby.gov.uk/leisureculture/museumsgalleries
Lowestoft Museum, Broad House, Nicholas Everritt Park, Oulton Broad,
Lowestoft, Suffolk NR33 9JR. Telephone: 01502 511457.
Museum of London, 150 London Wall, London EC2Y 5HN.
Telephone: 0870 444 3852. Website: www.museumoflondon.org.uk
Norwich Castle Museum, Castle Meadow, Norwich, Norfolk NR1 3JU.
Telephone: 01603 493625. Website: www.museums.norfolk.gov.uk
The Potteries Museum and Art Gallery, Bethesda Street, Hanley, Stoke-on-
Trent, Staffordshire ST1 3DW. Telephone: 01782 232323.
Website: www.stoke.gov.uk/museums
Spode Museum and Visitor Centre, Church Street, Stoke-on-Trent,
Staffordshire ST4 1BX. Telephone: 01782 572507. Website:
www.spode.co.uk/visiting_us/museum
Victoria and Albert Museum, Cromwell Road, South Kensington, London
SW7 2RL. Telephone: 020 7942 2000. Website: www.vam.ac.uk
Wedgwood Museum and Visitor Centre, Barlaston, Stoke-on-Trent, Staffordshire
ST12 9ES. Telephone: 01782 282818.
Website: www.wedgwoodmuseum.org.uk
Williamson Art Gallery and Museum, Slatey Road, Birkenhead, Merseyside
CH43 4UE. Telephone: 0151 652 4177.
Website: www.wirral.gov.uk
Worcester Porcelain Museum, Severn Street, Worcester WR1 2NE.
Telephone: 01905 746000.
Website: www.worcesterporcelainmuseum.org.uk

.1 3 NOV 2013

INDEX

Page numbers in italic refer to illustrations